MW00964921

REMNANT HALO

Also by Jon Curley

POETRY

New Shadows (2009)

Angles of Incidents (2012)

Hybrid Moments (2015)

Scorch Marks (2017)

CRITICISM

Poets and Partitions: Confronting Communal Identities in Northern Ireland

The Poetry and Poetics of Michael Heller: A Nomad Memory (Co-Editor with Burt Kimmelman)

Events and Victims by Bartolomeo Vanzetti (Editor)

REMNANT HALO

A Map N' Dice Chronicle

JON CURLEY

MARSH HAWK PRESS

East Rockaway, New York • 2021

Copyright © 2021 by Jon Curley

All Rights Reserved. No part of this book may be reproduced or utilized in any form or by any means, electronic or mechanical, including photocopying, recording, or by any information storage and retrieval system, without permission in writing from the publisher, unless faithfully conforming to fair use guidelines.

Marsh Hawk books are published by Marsh Hawk Press, Inc., a not-for-profit corporation under section 501(c)3 United States Internal Revenue Code.

Cover photograph: Jon Curley

Cover and book design: Hedi Allameh; copyright © Hedi Allameh 2021

FIRST EDITION

ISBN 978-0-9969912-4-7

Marsh Hawk Press
P.O. Box 206
East Rockaway, New York 11518-0206
www.marshhawkpress.org

ACKNOWLEDGEMENTS

Gratitude and Beatitude to Sandy McIntosh, Michael Heller, Jane Augustine, Burt Kimmelman, Kent Johnson, Lucas Swaine, Derek Coyle, Colin Flynn, Andrew Levy, Anthony Seidman, Kevin Bradbury, Chris Leo, Uncle Billy Christmann, Calista McRae, Kyle Riismandel, Pete Campbell, Tom Juvan, Dan Krugman, Gypsy James O'Toole, Pam LaMora, Eamonn Vitt, Zach Barocas, Ammiel Alcalay, Bob Singer, Miriam Ascarelli, Louise Castronova, Barbara Henning, Michael Patrick MacDonald, Ethan Goldberger, Leah Jackson, Eileen Mah, Donna Hartsoe, Garrett Caples, S. Mark Gubb, Ron Lembo, Kevin Curry, Dr. Larry Shemen, Michael Boughn, Alan Maimon, Brian Lucas, Kristin Prevallet, Pam Rehm, David Morwick, Victoria Livingtone, Marylou and Jerome Bongiorno, Bill Minor, Albert Mobilio, Ariana Curley, Geoff Curley, Tom Curley, and the Beauchamps.

Special thanks to Hedi Allameh, Elena Alexander, and Dan Morris.

This book is dedicated to my Fall 2020 poetry students. Verse Versus Virus!

In memory of Aurelio Parada (December 2, 1957-April 19, 2020) and in respect to the family he had to leave too early.

…Because the pandemic shreds and scrambles lives and maps while bringing wishes for navigation, both imagined and real and really imagined…thus:

pandemic = map n' dice

CONTENTS

REMNANT HALO

A Map N' Dice Chronicle

As the given groaned under the least contempt,

I faced again the lesion of the lesson and so

contained condemnation in the span of a mouth's

curse. Thirst: some habit of preferment despite

the shroud of environment, pitched here my tent

in the desiccated, rundown land, letting go of the

previous vision for this skewed scene and its

probable sequel as an even more damning

backdrop to future's controlling conceit.

Contempt. Effort to quell quandary of desire,

representation of that desire, the desire for

collective action. Contempt for cliché—

one's own—stuck, I am, in the syndicate of

previous signatures and registers, but mobilization

still desideratum lest half hope is deserted—and

then what suffices except hysterics, despair, or
worse? The effort to quell quandary as manifested
in the tawdry codes of tentative communication

when we are musing about optimal outcomes
or viable trajectories, where project 'demos'
grounds down, gets undone, becomes another

demic hostile to the harmonic or virtuous, the
collapse of the imaginary as Real roots out All,
rampant death designs whether etched into actual

daybook of this week's log or safe in storage
for next season's catastrophe. Wait and we
shall see, see saw, cast for prime portents

and stagger off into another enterprise
of calamitous divide with murderous dividends,
the congregants of disenchantment glow like

ghosts saturated in the alchemicals of heavy
industry. [Here, let us take pause to pattern
transition from global sentimental philosophy into

a more personal, gossipy litany of concerns, best
relayed with the sense that the particulars being
settled are being secured as sent testimonials, each

stanza a Post-it that gets posted and sent to you
over and over again.] So: The self swerved into a
semblance of self, not so much a steward of

percipience but an un-steward of emphatic tragic
stunted non-sense stark in its embarrassed antic
iteration. Soma in late Summer was a harbinger of

nerve-nettled autumn citizen, vitiating like those
misted vegetals, reminders that death-in-life is
veritable, our daily existence. Today is *Dies*

Laboris and work is nil for many across globe,

the coronal incursion setting the conditions

for the work of the imagination (the only work

not paralyzed by pandemic but struck mad

by it). The world that obtains accordingly

almost seems to command hermetic logic—

abrupt withdrawal from the horizon. Time

to put self in restraint, lock up in lockdown.

Spun breath in a skeleton, it seems. Gnawing

that nerve, seething and almost delirious

despite or because desultory days seem still

occasional in this museum and mausoleum

where light arranges its trickles like luminol

indicating that some crime(s) collect(ed) here.

When presented the evidence we still forewent

forensics and set off questing for amnesia
as our affordable, preferable utopia;
distraction from disruption, intersection

of futility with transit faith. My historical
trauma festered like a trash heap whose
pervading rot engulfed a world yet born.

Geometry of myth and method warped
so that those tufted wings of the sacred
technician, the Angel of History,

flew perforce vertically, beaten back
by the aggregate human waste
that was actually art forsaken for

state, translated into mere muddle, matter,
murder, the principle of hope
exploded, *urgrund* and *endziel*

confused, teleology now theology

of the cruelest kind of belief. No end.

Identity politics becomes tourniquet

Stanching spirit = "unhappiest religion

in the world." Anti-eidolon in a non-song

disappears through the flaps of the

unhappy maker's workshop where

wonders desist and wounds reve(a)l.

Simulacrum is now a shroud of original

sense. Intention wavers. Conceptual

currents not deep but sinking by the moment.

Boot-stamped faces now hard-won fashion

statement. Default fashion often the bruise

or tear flowering forth through our cosmetic

conversation—despite the lurking and

linking dangers. When precisely did
liturgies languish into threnodies?
When did the lists grow listless?

Calibration impossible. Cataclysm cost
analyzable? Not even dimly deducible.
We cannot withstand the spiritual losses

and all too many errands engineering
errors of attitude as well as action.
Crisis mode(m) now predominates

through the threshed body politic,
its tic is to harm both others and self
in a zero-sum game of persecution,

a trial vaccine of mercy not yet
developed to quell or kill it.
Oracular or miraculous mischief

should be our token vessels taken

as needed across obstructed space.

Under-determining any conceivable

action, an awestruck gnostic primer

to manage this mischief into macro-

particulates of joy-fretted *potentia*:

a fugitive faith pollinator to test

the solidity of convictions against

the quick shot default toward

the via negativa, that is, the bend

backwards, customary cul de sac

of analects retrograde, archive

curating what has not been made.

Instead of 'cul de sac,' why not

'coeur de sac' or, more properly

(but not entirely), 'coeur de sacri'?
Heart//Sacred//Sac red.
Why call on the sacred in this

September song? Why not?
Seeming specious categorical
imperative of awe in the guise

of holy ambit. Perhaps an affinity
not intended for us but needed no
matter. No matter. Still remainders

and reminders of the lives
that might have been. Still?
Every vision verges on collapse—

material and metaphor, those towers
felled nineteen years ago today.
Species specious, spectral,

living ghosts gasping,

grasping gospels, parchments,

parched earth where not scorched.

Out west the fires burning with

Blakean fury signal that 'climate

change' be rendered "climate

changed." Done deal. Death deal

the seal affixed to Gen Next

and thereafter and thereafter and later

and later it grows steadily the sense

we are situated on the encrusted cross-

beam of Purgatory and Horror Story

staggering through belief and unbelief

just beginning to assess the calamity

only now able to process the stages

of disfigurement that prevail upon

speech, song, spirit, and skin.

Where can I gather the voices

and storms needed to penetrate

the ache and make heritage

a healing fork attuned to harmonies

not yet heard but imagined? Mixed

miracles here I invoke as means of

avoiding the Official Verse Culture

penchant for simple sentiment,

spare image, casual utterance

or the freefall shattered sublime

of the ex-/peri-/ mental at the expense

of expressing the mess that this is:

the perpetual world we face

and the poetic mold that we model

as fragile, shy gesture of creation—

all a mess and a muck heap. Shit.

But what else is there? And what

is the language using us for?

Graham, dear cracker, W.S. (he is),

I still ask that and breathe badly

through my newly revised nose—

deviated nasal septum treated

and healing now (Thank you,

Dr. Shemen!) as now stark septums

sprawl across the territories,

tearing lands and lives, gashing

more hearts and grounds, forcing

us into artificial asymmetries of

geo-disparities, overseen by artisans

who wish most of us consigned

as mementos mori to dusted tracts

like Moria, now burned up, living

refugees' hell now vanquished. Readers'

comments today in the *NY Times* all

excoriated victims, for every such migrant

is a vagrant, not a victim, not even Other—

but object apt to blunt force instrument

at least in the improvident imagination

espoused by connoisseurs of casual cruelty

in their warped empaneled worlds. Grace

wears a gash in the tired spaces out there.

In here, the poem sets patterns akin

to gravesites or gardens in whose domains

grow both lush appeasements of the death-

dealing discourses and a blight contaminating

all fecund rhetorical roots. Are you still

still or do you tremble at the least speech

(the least speech)? Languish language,

and woe will grow in the wound of We.

That collective is various; here, the stance

struck is collective alignment, no political

consensus per se (and much silence),

a playing field engendering brave attempts, plenty

naïve and perhaps necessarily so,

of scanning sounds, senses, sentences,

rendering them into glorious, imperfect

structures of potent(ial) poetries

that stress the substance of irreverent

practices culminating in restorative

or transformative expressions, expressions

as incitements, fevers, forecasts, transcripts,

intercepts, and whatever nodes and modes

that can be mustered and delivered. Message

sent! This poetics mishmash maybe mis-

begotten but at least it's begetting mysteries

or the fragile envelope with which to send

them. Heritage commits progeny to vibrant

destiny and is the currency on which Tribe

tempers the disgust, anxiety, and menace

with exigent resolve, catapulting those poems

through those catastrophes and arranging

for a kind of renewal but of which kind yet

the muses are not kind enough to share.

But still we plot on and I have it on record

that furious Tinkerers among us (inscribed

in the Tribe) are making/doing what maybe

(constant conditionals!) will help treat

the infection that is the situation in which we

(barely) stand. Some of those operating little

theaters of resistance include Mike and Jane,

Kent and Brooks (pere & fils), Elena, Burt,

Fanny and Susan, Norman and Peter, Tyrone and

Joseph, Pam and Lew, Robert and Elizabeth,

Albert and John, Bill M., and Barbara H.,

also some of my student-poets waking

right now to form and possibility—to name

just a few—and so on…may the inventory

extend and bend the lines and broaden

the effects of verse as courage, corsage,
and curse—a valediction demanding more
singing! We want poems with teeth,

as Amiri B. urged then and so
we wish to peddle promiscuous fantasies
of poems with extra-textual vitalities! With

minds and fists! Ka pow! Whose fantasies?
Ours? No, mine, but this singular fantasy
is the ghost of orchestrated liberation

as opposed to incarcerated hibernation
in a cave or prison not our own. In coming
to terms with possession, we learn that

loss is another name for it, for we do not
possess any special claim to the lands
either grounded or texted. We just wander

here, there, and elsewhere, and try to put

our best enchanted feet first and fail again

and again as we are wont. Or will. Or won't.

Who will cry if we no longer raid the

particular, the inarticulate, find the means

to mess with the inauthentic? Let us

guess and meander, morph merrily

into a contracted partnership of 'You'

rather than 'We,' still plural and—

no, forget that adjustment, that frantic

conceit, and seek adjournment of any

move to puff and bluff for plurality

or profundity: no chance, any longer,

of that here. No reason now (as the mood

grows so goddamn dark I want to leave

this poem and whatever gestures it is

trying and failing —that word again—

('make') to do anything. Right. Got it.

But here is a new line and we addicts

have to approach it as a new day, new life;

this new line renews. And somehow some

of that alterna-song seems true. But not

proven. Contingent memory remedies

this reading, permits bypass of disaster

by dismantling it, shattering our once

shared sense that this necro-plane is the

endpoint and so then our only terrain

on which we can tread. Solace extends

to an isolated, subterranean track, obscured

by techno rites and media feeds,

a "through other" enfolded neatly in

the missive containing every first and last

line of the heraldic, hybrid international Epic

composed across countless cultures and

so many centuries by the Guild International,

authors, obscure and half known, together

elaborating a Perpetual People Verse

to displace the vermiform verbiages

prominent in our everyday squeal and spiel.

Dreamers can dream. And in Rojava, that

modest dream-territory of North and East Syria,

fragile yet firm, still the communal correlative

to this Poem as World Mover thrives

in spite of conflicts internal and exo-exacerbated.

Autonomous. Author. Autochthonous Authors

emerging from grounded legacies instead of
established academies. The Autodidact dedicated
to Art is no fiction: as Rimbaud's Face rode the

MTA, thanks to David Wojnarowicz's project, his
provision to make "I as Other," both himself
and not Self, Arthur Maudite and Arthur Made

Other, both done away, gone away, so damn
prematurely. I often pass DW's last residence on
the corner of East 12th Street and Second

Avenue, look up at his bedroom window and
wave a greeting thirty years too late. The plague
took him: "Dying is a mirror expressed in

artifices." D was a Poet as well as a Painter,
Prophet too. Pandemic paraclete, Sage of Rage,
you would stand indignant as virus vectored

across the globe abetted by emissaries of

ignorance and mortality reducers, would defy

the tide and stand not for the mayhem

moving across and through us, in us too. Amens

over mayhems, praise be the solar plexus placed

prayer, prayer the soma errata that may yet

move mouths into configurations congenial

to grace. Grace: the grace race still instructs

space. Let us now resurrect the representation,

if not the thing itself, of pilgrim's progress in

the form of a remnant halo, shared by

disintegrating persons and jellyfish, each fortified

by the fierce, frantic gesture towards renewal

while uncertain futures await on either shoreline

or soul side. Earlier today, the soul of struggle

lustrated in the gallery at the Met where
Jacob Lawrence's *American Struggle* exhibition
unrested, writhing with ecstatic and subversive

energies, blending and bleeding the citizens
and slaves and citizen slaves in vivid
senses/scripts/fields (art during plague is

revelation; history's plague inscribes disease
deep in the human family's reservoir: never
revelatory, but reveals surely the crude

cataclysm of our community initiatives,
at least most of them). Lawrence's Law
unfolds the Edict of Activism and Black

Lives Matter in colors that ripen, reel,
and rage (that word again, this age in need
of it so resolutely) and the black figures

seem semaphores calling for—then

and now—another possible relation—

challenging state and psyche, making way

for harmonic heritages where struggle

lives on as competition to establish

the utmost compassion. But I am jumping

far beyond the paintings' frames, am

in fact creating a jumble of images, light

shows, fragile hopes that a poem can only

futilely fathom in the little rooms it adds

to itself and accretes down the page,

slivers of life that beckon at oblivion

and break badly as any obscure self

in the *selva oscura* of lyric arbors shall,

despite the urge to go on. I must go

on to the terrain of trusts that imparts

protectorate status to the imagined glory

of greater world(s?) possible. Then

I am thrust off the poetic track

as the death toll due to this virus

exceeds 200,000. Elegy, I elude

your properties in coming to grips

with these numbers in this makeshift

Underworld that visited us, not vice versa.

No guide to govern heart tremors or

statistical breakdowns; led by the hand,

the soul breaks off, a procession of dead

that cannot be accurately processed,

grief trials hover over the autumnal months,

pall casting down is covered in toxic chemicals

that dying generations will feature in their end-
songs, savoring the full-throated shriek across
the tundra only barely realized as personally

voiced, not echo, not memory. The horror.
But there is another cry, another call to order,
license to vacate abyss-abode, resist that

"pre-invented world" (thank you, David W.!)
and contrive new chartings, voicings,
vatic field operations to evoke escapist yet

confrontational settings and secure
that paradise invoked under an infant's
eyelid, waiting for its transmission

into the collective witness box
of an early spring (in feeling, if not season).
Obsequies will never grow obsolete and those

shadows will sustain, setting forth

from the constant stream of terrors, so

too the trip-wires of confounded spirit

and those dark thoughts pressurized

in Skull, the old relic box. Gather

graces and forces (this autosuggestion

arranges itself like gauze on wounded

psyche) and suppose that trauma just might

alter, not just alleviate, leaving us sad still but

not disconsolate, ever ready to engineer

methods mixed with magic and conjoined

with practice to advance a New Ark

(as ecumenical as my eye) to strike

forth. And out. These lines are composing

in Newark, New Jersey, as the sun sets

down on the first day of fall, not the

first day of The Fall. This city was founded

a year before *Paradise Lost*, proleptic,

retrospective, purgatorial city,

your residents reside in me, at once so

beleaguered and yet bold, attractive

in that manner reserved for the coolest

derivations of art genius germinating

from the streets and city walls. Go with me

now with ghosts accumulated over

many walks across these desolate

avenues, raked by overhead surveillance

lights mimicking foundry furnace

spark signatures signing into the gloom.

Now swerve: compose in darkness

and rearrange one's brain to harness

the recognition of too many ruins, and

repose not. I embrace swervings as

only antidote for direct sense assaults

so am now moving on. If you could join me

in this poem I would be less forlorn,

forward footed, and exact. But now

vagaries and vagueness pervade and

stymie whatever counter-trends I might

attempt to make. To make: only form

of control or resistance these or any days.

Autumn abolishes absolutes or any slight

redemptive pulse when eyeing evidence

so caustic and enormous. Details defy

imagination in their onslaughts or else

parse particulars so strenuously that
they tend to bleed facts and flower
frustration. More strenuous than

the flu, so it was dubbed around
Valentine's, seemingly pre-p
time. 'Valen-time': sacred scope

of agapé epoch against this agony
season. Just announced: NYC homeless
relocated uptown now thrown downtown.

Poverty, poetry, everything in tatters.
Ill-gotten gains glossed by garish
sentiment (I am sorry). Rights

aborted, abortion rights, contortion
consciences, distortion sites. Concentrate.
Concentration. Camps. Dispersals of

references and refugees. The ethics
of an 'Amen'…the wherewithal to not
grieve so prodigiously on the tenth

anniversary of her passing. Amen, Ma,
I am inscribing you in me, in this poem
while plague perseveres. Never will I

sever that vein that merges me with you.
That menacing mood of *Octoberisme*
this year will bring me to the brink,

breaking point, whatever descriptor
debases the real and clichés abound
to be harvested and heaped as they

are, as they are. Thwarts and all.
Elegy for ebb—and so much besides.
Distress signals _____? Remember

'Assassin poems'? They had been sent.

Why not havens instead of warrens?

In this Great Clinical Depression

any sanctuary might suffice. The call

for a Working Class Action has still

to be made. Over there, in the declining

sun-bathed glow, across the East River,

the combined industrial and rampant

residential complexes seem etched

and issued by Tintoretto. Still, art balm

transports the unaccommodating universe

into an unlikely but deeply felt fissure

in which pours resplendent vital fluid

of elsewhere and otherwise. This escape,

this transfusion, of course requires

deep contact with the here and now.

Constant. This flâneur has been stopped

in his tracks. "Keep it going!" I hear

my mother intone but spiritual paralysis

has a way of freezing the feet and mind.

Overhead, hawks circle in demented concentric

and recently Tu Fu encouraged me to read

those wings as synergies of menace. Those

birds do not reel so much but they are indignant

there in the glacial deserts of the air. My ear

listens for ancestors resting in molecules

moving through me and offering votives

during virus in the shape of prophecy,

the heft of which I cannot lift yet. The said

reckoning with atmosphere has me

still eating clouds of unknowing but

still insisting (the 'I' within the 'I')

that something has got to give way.

Turning eyes inward indicates

the muddled habitus of subconscious:

not one dream of any resolution

has drifted through me since March.

Stagnant pools, funereal fundaments

litter the mindscape except rare bursts

of agonized, attempted processing which

only happens by the coronal day light. Mission

creep has increased the causality of anxiety

headaches and whiskey-swilling sham-

anistic late night antics, a sham really,

for all I or this poem can predict may

be a slightly false witness to the misery-
en-scène. Turn those whispers into vespers
and may those prayers into which I enter

deliver domains of strategic (w)reck-
oning that myself did impart. Worship houses
are now contamination corridors, reinforcing

the hard-to-breathe atmosphere, almost
giving halation effect to suffering in extreme
devotion. Breathing as prayer—meditation

states, viral verse as apotropaic, death-defying
insurgents. Oh, the flights so desperate and
bright, like miracle zones of repose (that

word again!). Clutching hair, branches, roots
become daily exercises of holy hospice
care. But I cannot fully embrace any

cant or creed (or can't I?) that fails

(all belief fails) to keep the coda

clear for 'Non serviam' and see(r)

you later. Vision veers and vaults,

seeks higher orders, callings,

across thresholds seeking holy

presences, soaring, no matter

what; yes, they are there, though

the retro rule, runs the refrain, is that

Angels and Saints are figments—

But they are fragments, too,

and I shall tether my talisman

to their multifarious forms

and wing it (Eliot Weinberger

sings it in a book just published

by New Directions). Behold:

angels at work for ora et labora!)

Ora-laboratory! o + l = call to arms,

hearts, crosses, minds, modest attempts

at self-revision—the alchemical compound

is ecumenical, to be sure. Salve-ation:

Is it worth the effort of extraction?

Halo not yellow but the Post-it placed

there at eye-level for years reads:

"Mi vida ha sido como una farsa."

And so it has, along with surges, shudders,

so many stricken-seizing upticks that surpass

my understanding. That splinter in my eye…

There, now, a landscape art reveals

just ruckus, some ruins, and an isolato

sewing his own garment on the murky margins

of an unknown expanse. You know this image

to be a mirror and you are wrenched into

seething attitudes. Feel the impulse

to jump, and the balcony is fifteen floors

up from Second Avenue. Infrequently,

a nocturnal gliding dive into the street

has been the pathetic fallacy, pathetic

non-action, of the reimagined me. Last

time I thought (ha!) of depths-retreating

maneuvers marking the pavement with

my person was—"Yakarta Viene"?—

when that unmarked police car disappeared

the demonstrator. But that mark would be

neither me nor poem's flare, no, a rock

fired down and against those badged brutes,
not one masked, tasked to tread boot on face
for future reference of our temporally tipped

pandemic most powerfully policed. Snipped
collective cortical knot. It figures that most
books of enchantment a.k.a. our incitement texts

lay fallow on their bookshelves, spines
aligned like ours, a lateral languishing. Ethical
distancing, a serene surrender to the factitious

freeze. Ode, I drive mischief up your sleeve
and plunge it down into this paper ground
while running red and rampant to an exit door.

Did I read about Covid empathy fatigue?
Affect be ambient, be the Arch Leavener to lead
species into rising patterns. Declension has too

long been a factor, face lowers at impending

downwards. Turn-It-Kits are needed

after the tourniquets are removed. Also

errant passage into off-chance agendas.

But enough rampant speculation on

material and spiritual probabilities

(being pro-babble-idiocies I so

commonly cling)—back to the daily

brain consignment to immediacies

and their decisive agonies: Were it

not for the gift of solace sought

so recklessly through the examples

of all those metaphysical brawlers,

in one form or another (poetic

or familiar or both), thereby

boosting my immune system

for fighting off the malefactors

who no longer hide and hit and

hit. They know who they are

even if they are long dead precedents

who never laid eyes on me yet

continue to saunter past me.

Those angles of light? Those are them.

Why even in a poetic journey does exhaustion

set in before the first stanza is leapt out of?

Imagine what the reader must feel (simpatico

automatico) and you plunder on in a plague

pilgrimage, homage to all non-Puritan

ego-agog seekers staggering across these

blasted heaths filled with so many blasted

lives. Reminded of that terrifying tag
line from that 80's Italian demon
flick: "They will make cemeteries

their cathedrals and the cities will
be your tombs." Brrr. Why is it that
schlock best captures the spirit

of real sites, the coordinates of our
catastrophes? So many losses,
varieties of despair, misery mires

along with those strangleholds
of sadness. Neither not there nor
not there. Mass migrations, internal

and far-flung. Not enough subjects
sung; they carry on. Invaders?
No, usually cadavers, with a ground-

swell of contempt for them who
are also us. Yes. Shhh. More thoughts
release more shame. Help us, saviors,

whoever you are. Might be. Modern
psycho-geography adverts to mass
hysteria of the *historia* kind, and that

seems just so right—because, again—
so wrong. The medium of lament, so
clogged with over-use, now drones

on at a queasily constant clip,
only foundering into silence when
its instrumentalists expectorate

blood issuing from others. Then
that familiar thrum starts up again,
commingling with other murder melodies,

sounds of razor propellers, downloading

software files, heavy metal artillery,

the grim din of our swan song swooning

a soon-to-be long sonata of the dead.

Perhaps we awaken and transcend end

(though transcend has an end in it),

coming not to our senses but seeking

those senses far away, a voyage from here

into untested tracks (some monks from

Clonmacnoise in their marvel mobilization

might have beaten most of us). So many

of us have been beaten, my God, the punishing

intention is so dexterous and the default

for it a seduction of power for the sake

of gathering sadism's portfolio. Atrocity

exhibitions now showcased with pride

throughout countries referred to

as First/Second/Third Worlds but

really all Underworlds in degrees

of reliable dark agonies (so too those

intermittent seas). Violence is a virus too

(no vaccine discovered for all ages)

erupting in both belligerent blasts

and oh-so-subtle gentle applications

(Did you feel that? I know you did).

Contingent freedom comes with

green thoughts. Bower memory.

The nettles in my neck stir,

so too the brambles arrayed under

scalp, vegetal visions make sight

an optic greenhouse rooted

in a holy rood trans/planted

and infused in the cruciform thoracic

shelf that has developed in/for me.

Amen! Shelf discovery. Self discovery.

Covid discovery. Dis-Covid Condensary:

Not a Baedecker needed, always a Niedecker!

Plots always thicken into sloughs of

narrative desponds—now, especially—

so may the fractured passage we embark

encourage the onslaught of non-plots,

poetic place markers, to enhance pop-up

funhouses incumbent on *eros* so eroded

in the punishments of present. Diversions

are ad hoc alleviators, I know, but any presto

chango gimmicks are preferable when

every day becomes astringent rebuke

to any hope-not-harm might muster.

How perilous is it, in fact or fiction,

dear Seamus, to choose not to love

the life we're shown? What had been

shown to you was certainly enough

for you to be like Sweeney, astray,

or Willie and his hammered metal

Byzantium bird fantasies: the desire

to get out of this place, if it's the first

or last thing that we do. With your assent

and example, I grow wings, not

angelic, for elsewhere flights. I seek

the air for respite from this raw realm

where only ill will and winds register

and nightly my terrors tremble beneath

their abettors, that is, the evidence of this

infernal world-maze with no way out!

Just now, as that previous stanza solidified

(but as the inspiration for it curdled like

almost all of my ideas or theories or poems

into nacreous nonsense), I remembered

how that starving woman reminded me

that obedience to the laws of gravity

was/is/will be the greatest sin. Merci,

Simone, I still relish you, relict, your

edict to embrace emphatically the hole

through which trickles the holy gives

me such ego assassination and also

keeps me whole. During Covid, I
must become, at least in these leased
words, Corvid, and fly now not away

but above, casting light, lies, both
filaments of grace and disgrace as
I fumble in flight for a flight track

that might be right. Or so fantastically
wrong that it amounts to the same
place (your preferred sub- or ob-

ject here, in conjecture). Remember,
it is so important to clarify and announce
yourself, as my fellow poets moon-

lighting as Louisville policeman did
when they (are we really here again
at the scene of another...? Fuck!)

shot our sister and got away with it?
I go away from it, all of it, and peck
at our collective soul. After all, this

Curley Corvid curlew creature flies
in the face of his own face. Always.
Then I took a here-and-not-here

investigative odyssey and felt
all my possible brains record ecstasy
and then plunge into whatever extremes

you have always commended as needed.
Bleeded. Blooded. Some ways, flooded—
estuaries as new access points, replenish

this blood, this body, and go forth, glide on...
as against suspension, this seeming aberrant
abeyance, intensification not abatement,

'pandemic intelligence' barely coherent,

almost obscene. Why do the pre-viral

and mid-outbreak outrages seem to slip

away, leak away into the media maelstrom

(You know to which I refer) and will

deliverance clarify the contours of

this broken (sinking?) world? View.

Review. Requiem request. Coroners'

Reports, all of them, please smuggle

them out and let us read the inventory

as means to reinvent our history. May

testimonies garland our anxieties, thwart

arguments that dismantle credible action—

no reversal or return but invigorated

gestures. Faith and mercies as essential

investments in these future matters

(faith as framework for matter). Did you

approximate prayer in your entire

relict self? Do you now? May facts

pronounce you 'led.' Me, too. Plurality

of Amens in the glare of this autumn

day. Echoes of Celan's "Corona"—

"…consented to bloom/a heart beat for unrest/

It's time it came time." Thin thought,

with a shudder cries out: "Not yet." Sunspots

or tears in corrective lenses lending nimbus-

like shape on the complex across Second Avenue.

I go searching for signs and keep reading

into somber shadows signatures of surprise,

omens of authentic angelic enterprise

(code for world and word apocalypse).

engaging *gematria*, deliberating divine

sparks, poetry by other means but still

in the spirit of diverse faiths, *faits divers*,

in deep harmony with the h(a)unted,

incomplete heritage of domain-defying,

red and black agitations. Traditions. Behold!

Be holy in assuming a universal grammar

where sectarianism specters are squashed

by propellants of communal activation

(these solidarities can be contagious, too).

Am thinking of smaller graces too

that dwell in soul-site repositories

offering celebration and collaboration

like Samuel Menashe's mentoring marvels

and his Machado version inked

into my copy of his *To Open*:

"Now spring has come/No one

Knows how." Revelatory, gnostic

spring sentiment for this frantic fall,

momentary succor. Now that moment over.

Gallivant and keep it slant, I tell self,

and make oblique run against routine

while keeping a grace space for ritual:

mark days, take breath, write poems

as messenger service giving meaning

over menace to part-owner, part passerby

(the poem refuses utmost ownership).

Standby: the errant, antic poetic avatar

just turned and shook off any contagion-by-present, confronting earth agonies

and passed off into wish-wonder then

prayer for mass *metanoia*. Moving from

poem to city view, perspective gets engulfed

by deserts, vast desolate tracts, where

citizens used to mass, near where 800+

were dying every day. April's cruelest.

Even with traffic moving, inertia seems

affixed to every surface, system, star.

Or maybe projection of inner to outer

inveigles unholy sight? Blind spots

everywhere. Fugitive moods maroon

me on the threshold of prospect and

despair, visions busted into shifting

mosaics, the fragmented scenes fusions

of present and past tableaus, scenarios.

Need an echo chart from some phantom

cartographer to realign mission with motion,

sails shredded, storms permanently threaten.

Homeland now seems so abstract, so untrue,

as untenable as calling the air clean or those

distant islands reachable. If I could just

navigate my own twin sense of faith and doubt,

discount those shoals, surfs, and surges,

I might be able to make my way by way

of byways laid by better souls and coordinate

congregants around me. Most magicians of space

are women so I endorse the feminine fork

in the formation of travel tendencies. May

their models guide me. Here I go—not there

or here, that elsewhere always sought
and shared regardless of whatever itineraries
assumed. So onwards we tread, sending forth

illuminated paths on which to depart. Journey
future-tense will be shot through with residues
of previous views in anticipation of never-before

shores. Anti-migrants will mock us and mark us
as we proceed. Garden-like calentures grip our
sights and already the calendars have been ripped

down. Ghost ships for the living, we realize that
all preparation for an exit expedition has been
harried into purpose and reverie by onslaught

after onslaught, pandemic particulates
toxifying brain stem. Stranded again
one can only sing farewells to several

dead selves, immaculate mental shrouds

left hanging on the previous era—in sin

domes amid syndrome. Sun on spire,

Church of the Epiphany, late afternoon.

Harvest light filtering over all: Severe,

acute. Respite for respiratory, reading

Dante, catching my breath, wishing

to glimpse *stelle* instead of imagining

pandemic stelae littering this century.

Seeing stars, seeing SARS, swiftly

Summoning also Swift (namesake, practically

 co-spirit this season): "Such order from

confusion sprung…" If only.

Disruption and decay order day after day until

time tunnels under coherence. Correspondent

loosening of logic but inability to distinguish

whose. Project of coming to terms. Wandering

souls and waiting spirits readjust their meandering

streams. On these city streets, one can no

longer determine whether pandemic pilgrims

mimic their previous personalities or else

saturate roving selves with sanitizers

that cleanse epidermis and bewilderment

simultaneously. Calling all curiosity seekers!

Does pain produce immunity for humanity's

penchant to endeavor horror all too often?

Holy levitation! That is a questing question

indeed. Unanswerable? That is…

Haunted by the future, into which I add

dire readings ruining any possible narrative

not unsettling. Haunted by the present,

through which I pass from one zone of

hazy deliberation into a confusion bank

beset by all those familiar fears. Tensions

wire the brainpan to contagion conceits.

Profound gloom before evening. *Night*

Philosophy, I've been reading, by Fanny Howe,

published just as this virus hit. How

distant are theological compounds

and epidemiological ones, when

the body holistically is heralded

and examined? The nurses, doctors,

and orderlies all look like pastel cenobites

coming off their shifts. What rituals were

conducted with open codices, cannulas,

ministries of incredible resolve. Spirit

much moved, I worship thee. Trying

to translate the weight of circumstance

into an inhabitable hurt. Not working.

Everywhere I am invaded by absence.

Will definitely call my father tonight

as last night I was out assembling new

poets to guide them, however remotely,

into the body of work. Into the wreckage.

Despair (again, that word), I'll feast on you

and think of comfort, carrion, fell dark,

obituary as intensification of presence—

yours, GMH (God/Man/Hope?), dead of

typhoid, buried in Glasnevin Cemetery

where adjacently I commemorated you

at John Kavanagh's Gravediggers' Pub

along with Hedi and Eoghan. Then there's

Grey Space a.k.a. Gg Re a.k.a. Gregory

Spector (a real poet InSpector!), dead at 47,

and ash-scattered. Even younger, Olivia Barker

borne into afterlife at 40, talented, lamented,

gone without me telling her how much she

meant to—what? Threnodies spin wildly

across the song spectrum. Sadness consumes

like cancer so stuck in the cell prison of

our communal compartment. You just

wish for that revenge of redemption, some

maneuvering cleared of this too. Yes,

redemption is thorough revenge for the

infinite unfortunate occurrences that cling

to us like sin, conscience, burrs, shackles,

faiths, whatever we animals deem or declare

pan-demonic debacle of the always. Eternity

eats my wounds, true and eventual, eventually.

Every day, my daughter teaches me

that digression and revision are the keys

of sustaining light, structure, sanity, self,

so I shall concur with her and train my sights

on those sites, those illusory islands upheld

by the soul that inspires and respires, performing

both effectively without hindrance or pause.

Tender tendrils arisen from revolutionary roots

of children in change-desiring sodalities

of solidarities do these days encourage

the onwards atmospheres of keep-going

considerations (She just shook her head
to confirm. Thank you, ABC! We must
make a fist and move future-forward

as what other options do we have?) Sail
to Byzantium by the seat of our...what?
Ok, let us press the imaginary button

and now escape imaginatively—for a spell—
then move back into ground zero, apropos
of everything. Stand your ground now

has a different meaning. Necessarily so.
Repetition and near-simulation have crept
into this poem, too numerous to displace;

I shall apologize and yet not quite retreat
from those repeats, gifts of remembered
positions and failed new conditionals—

liberation through repetition? A call

to disorder, sound the alarums. When

action seems inadequate, raise a new

slew of questions and plunge them hard

into the ground. There, quandaries will

grow but so too nascent notions offering

their branches (later, when matured). Threats

of surges encircle, factions enflame, such

fracturing of the biosphere. What happened

(t)here? Writing the disaster differs drastically

from describing the monstrous. This latter is a

lesson in lesion and in/cohesion. It is happening

here, real passions impoverished beyond

comprehension. 'Give me more understanding'

can never be overstatement, basking

in the glow of my own ignorance. One can

almost be considered mystical about so

much of this infected world's prospects—

can't find much faith in theorizing any

shred of what is to come. Wheat-pasted

poster this morning encourages EMPATHY

while beside it a black scrawl to "Repent!"

Pestilential, penitential, we all feel the down-

ward drift. Reason for always looking skyward?

This Friday sky-scapes are Burnt Elysiums

and recall again Blake in page and paint.

This holiday weekend haunted by myth

of discovery and we need some discovery

myth to set ablaze our dim daily scene.

Demented demesne run by futile feudalists,

portions of it in flames, I plead for water

and sanity, and cite these developments

as elemental shames. Elsewhere, however,

excess floods and ruins over all. Terror

of error: the greater terrain refuses

homeostasis because we, too, disclaim

any reduction of extremes into inventions

of balances, comforts, or eases. Only sieges

metastasize in mental states, so I plead

for Heaven's gate or at least a heart

referendum rendering ruin into restoration.

In this hope puzzle heap, I am (all) alone.

But I, too, connive in unhelpful, mad,

even murderous dreams—deliver us from

them, let us pray. Knelt because taking

a knee seemed prayer and a humbling,

ritual of restraint. May they too know

who they are and what they do. Blue

is the color of their sin, black the sheen

of possibility, inside and outside the skin.

Mad madrigal I compose improvised on

night walk, observe shuttered storefronts,

looming figures, mostly drifting vagrants.

Of these I sing, and cherish faces I encounter

even when they wear masks of oblivion. Our

decision to sing in spite; grief weavers worded

with the woe and wreck soundtrack of state.

Every distance desires path-purgatories

and we swoon in these side-ways as inadequate

but necessary crossings and trackings, tracing

the traffic of our left lives even as
we evade them. Stagger on, word,
would I make new land off this shore

while summoning new patterns
to guide me and speak in. The vale
of tears never resides far enough

and veils my eyes in lamentations.
Suspended in air: my thoughts, my tears,
droplets not of rain. Confounding,

conflicting evidence, speculation.
A speck. Am I. Memory agog,
its uplift abilities gone ages ago.

Not sure what form the grail will take
these times, where buried, when buried.
Burnished and emblazoned, yes, still

I have a romance of redeeming themes:
Space space interface grace. Bend and bow,
accede to the worshipful, be bettered

even if battered. The letter bespeaks
truth to be told, wrecking world willed.
May those metaphysical brawlers not

cease in their antic operations; over
there, that cornerstone looks like a
cross. The homeless look like pilgrims

enduring pogroms, our failed programs.
Desired outcomes despite denials;
an entire demographic theorized

for oblivion. Focus group forbidden,
stricken people emerge from sidewalks
and holes they are assigned and menace

any ease of civic sort. Imaginary island, I land

on you and commence a pursuit of new

collective real estate expectations. The other

day, I saw a sign downtown that my mind

revised visually, methodically, so then there

came an ode and a refrain, a hinge and

a hook, the sign then realized more than

mere words in some real/m of the con-

ceivable: ***NO PRIVATE P(R)O(P)E(R)TR Y!***

(Carry that exclaiming down and onwards,

why not?) Note the symphony of probable

lyrics does not yet cast us out of the Book

of Life? We cannot not pray nor yet steer

past pressure and strife. I recall the gardens

of the Poets in Shiraz, Iran, festooned

with families, poets, and the ardently endeared.

Gaia and dialectics must pulse green blood

into the next chapters unless we await erasure.

I am amazed and drained at once; I fear

the failed faculties of our predicaments. Why

is the air so energetic with/for our elimination?

Every young person fills me with holy heat.

I might not live long enough to _____?

Can we assemble a congress of true concordance?

Vertigo is the emblem of ego in this season

of tumult, assault, desuetude, and proper

or improper attitude. The workbook of woe

has been ours and has been hard won. Stunned.

So 'sinned' may be wrong but it might be a right

(the Moralist must give way to the Miraclelist)

as we hold and head on. I cannot assume

we all are Wandering Mourners but so many

of us are. I am with you, if you know what

I tried to mean over these words, over

these years. Nothing much matters now

that you have fled on pilgrimage into

the deepest recess of my heart. Some words

and shadows cause me to tremble. I am

sorry and stare at the stars in stupefaction.

There arose, this rose, that rising of—so

many flowers and fumes considering, con-

sidered, propulsion and propellants, that raw

poetry and vagrancy of spirit that show we

meant so much even if we could not express it.

Forgive us or me or you. Not trying to implicate,

maybe imply, or explain: that old refrain:

stoppeth one of three, as in the Trinity,

as in you and me and We. Let us commence

to render the repentance as a path to

commitment not commonly espoused.

Looking towards those island ideals,

mirages hovering like x-ray plates

above my life, across terrain too terrible

to describe except as reels of memory film

I try to store in an attic or trap door

adjacent to a precinct of Nevermore.

May the days swell and release us

into a new habitat unhindered by

the despots of dire dispensation.

The *tractatus* I want to write would invoke

that ancient tradition and otherwise

experimental rendition of psalm. Balm.

Despite all my furies and infirmities, I

am devotee, devotional to another way

beyond this path. Route out of death's

head into the realm of dreaming purposes.

Route out of here. See you later, see you

now? Some nature notaries append this note

to the voice caught in the spokes of its own

spoke. Learning how to lessen the losses

while also counting them: pandemic

arithmetic: 1-2-200,000-???? Please, end.

How did we land here, stranded, bereft

on edge, at edge, at the end of the page?

Follow the >>>>>>>>>>>>> o

Notes:

17: **_urgrund_ and _endziel_"**: "primordial cause" and "end goal" borrowed along with principled hope and with reverence, from Ernst Bloch, preferred teleologist.

18: **"unhappiest religion in the world"**: Musician Nick Cave's coinage for political correctness in issue #109 of _The Red Hand Files_, August 2020, in response to the question: "What do you think of cancel culture?"

18: **"Boot stamped faces"**: from George Orwell's _1984_: "If you want a vision of the Future, imagine a boot stamping on a human face—forever."

24: Echoes **W.S. Graham's** "What Is The Language Using Us For?" from _Malcom Mooney's Island_ (1970).

32: **"through other"**: Northern Irish poet W.R. Rodgers's phrase from "Armagh."

37: **"as the death toll due due to this virus/ exceeds 200,000…"**: September 21, 2020, day before Fall.

38: **"pre-invented world"**: David Wojnarowicz's

phrase for the brutal reality of life that art and deep perception can challenge. Wojnarowicz: "I am trying to lift off the weight of the pre-invented world so I can see what's underneath it all."

39: **"Skull, the old relic box"**: phrase from Michael Heller's "Eschaton."

40: **"[C]ompose in darkness"**: phrase from Seamus Heaney's "North."

44: **"Assassin Poems"**: from Amiri Baraka's "Black Art."

49: **"That splinter in my eye"**: gestures toward Adorno: "The splinter in your eye is the best magnifying glass" (from *Minima Moralia*, re-read during pandemic). Also instructive, if one is honest about pandemic and poems, is this sentence from same volume: "True thoughts are those alone which do not understand themselves."

50: **Yakarte Viene**: "Jakarta is Coming." Cards sent to Chile's Allende government officials with these words and graffiti in Chile with this slogan appeared just prior to the 1973 coup by Pinochet; it refers to the state terror of Suharto in Indonesia.

54: **"that 80's Italian demon flick":** Lamberto Bava's *Demons* (1985).

56: **"long sonata of the dead":** from Beckett's *Molloy*:

59: **"...to choose not to love the life we're shown":** the phrase is taken from Seamus Heaney's "The Badgers."

70: **"Such order from confusion sprung":** from Jonathan Swift's "The Lady's Dressing Room."

78: **"Burnt Elysiums":** phrase from Patrick Pritchett's "Orphic Noise" published in *Hambone 22.*

85: **"Follow the...":** Code: perhaps suggesting a spiritual and social future leading to an ascendant halo/holy metaphor for collective experience...otherwise menacing indicator of a collective trapdoor through which We All Fall Through...

...

Endtro:

Far from being a *Confessio*, this work is mostly a *Confusio*, an ardent yet failed attempt to come to terms with the haphazard thought and experience that have denied me a stable place in the world.

A profusion of confusion has inundated me since March 2020 and I figured I should display and splay it, all the while trying to, at the same, reclaim some personal territory of coherence and clarity in the process. I have largely failed, an enduring objective whatever the given effort.

In early September 2020, I put aside a manu-script-in-the making and turned to this project. The inspiration was exhaustion, so too that domi-nating state of confusion that stoked resentment. Whenever my students asked me how I was feel-ing or how I was doing, I would inevitably reply: "I don't know. I cannot process any of this." I am still, prosaically and psychologically speaking, that vast clotted cloud of unknowing. However, the practice of poetry helps me translate that un-knowing into certain provisional notions, senti-ments, reflections, and commentaries.

In this long poem I have strived to be radically honest to myself and to my potential readers. In this document is a lot of doubt but also heaps of faith, rage and lament, striking love and smiting hatred. None of these words do justice to this work but this work seeks justice for this world. It is still waiting for it.

This pandemic has only revisited many of the well-lighted chambers and too-dark habitats of our human society, forever embattled by viral and vital forces, emanating from elsewhere and deep in ourselves. Mapping routes through a pandemic world and all the contingency involved in living or thinking through it is encoded in the scrambling of the subtitle: pandemic = map n' dice.

This volume was written with the hope that poetry could be a site of stability, a repository of trauma, but also a powerful, multifaceted prayer. It was modeled after the old Irish voyage narrative, the *immram*, showcasing travels to Underworlds and Otherworlds. Throughout the past year, we all have visited these other worlds without having left our own.

The tone of *Remnant Halo* can be dark so the poem's structure can be said to resemble the architectural form of *confessio*—interlocking crypt passages, stanzas as crypts.

But there is another abiding influence and it also has Irish roots: "In the beginning was the pun…" This quotation from Samuel Beckett's 1937 novel *Murphy* is in some ways a foundational source of inspiration for this work. Often, recourse to punning was for me and these words a coping mechanism, image generator, and concept creator. The puns abounding here mean serious business.

While the references in this long poem are almost exclusively male and predominantly Irish, the resonant Muse and Mobilizer, in keeping with the *immram* enterprise and impetus, is female and pi-

ratical. This work casts itself adrift in the name of
Gráinne Ní Mháille (c.1530-c.1603) who still sails
the sacred seas rebelliously and redemptively. She
and so many Rebel Grrls, Irreverends, and exper-
imental wanderers inspire, provoke, and protect.
They shadow this text decisively.

The frequent mention of faith acts almost as a
stuttering machine, a willed and needed affir-
mation of faith as a trademark of personal and
communal identity. It is less a nod in any religious
direction but is absolutely a summoning of spiri-
tual force. We need that force now and ever.

+ + + + +

Draft Completed: October 20, 2020
(U.S. Coronavirus deaths: 211,846
 people...)

First Revision: January 19, 2021
(U.S. Coronavirus deaths today exceed
400,000 people...)

Final Revision: March 1, 2021
(U.S. Coronavirus deaths today exceed
513,000 people...)

In Incertum Spiritus >>>>>>>>>>>>>>

About the Author:

Jon Curley is also the author of *Scorch Marks* (2017), *Hybrid Moments* (2015), *Angles of Incidents* (2012), and *New Shadows* (2009). Originally from New England, he now resides in New York City. A professor in the Humanities Department of New Jersey Institute of Technology, he counts poet Amiri Barka and the citizens of Newark, New Jersey as particular inspirations.

Visit his website at: www.joncurley.com

Titles From Marsh Hawk Press

Jane Augustine *Arbor Vitae; Krazy; Night Lights; A Woman's Guide to Mountain Climbing*

Tom Beckett *Dipstick (Diptych)*

Sigman Byrd *Under the Wanderer's Star*

Patricia Carlin: *Original Green; Quantum Jitters; Second Nature*

Claudia Carlson *The Elephant House; My Chocolate Sarcophagus; Pocket Park*

Meredith Cole *Miniatures*

Jon Curley *Hybrid Moments; Scorch Marks*

Neil de la Flor *Almost Dorothy; An Elephant's Memory of Blizzards*

Chard deNiord *Sharp Golden Thorn*

Sharon Dolin *Serious Pink*

Steve Fellner *Blind Date with Cavafy; The Weary World Rejoices*

Thomas Fink *Selected Poems & Poetic Series; Joyride; Peace Conference; Clarity and Other Poems; After Taxes; Gossip*

Thomas Fink and Maya D. Mason *A Pageant for Every Addiction*

Norman Finkelstein *Inside the Ghost Factory; Passing Over*

Edward Foster *A Looking-Glass for Traytors; The Beginning of Sorrows; Dire Straits; Mahrem: Things Men Should Do for Men; Sewing the Wind; What He Ought to Know*

Paolo Javier *The Feeling is Actual*

Burt Kimmelman *Abandoned Angel; Somehow*

Burt Kimmelman and Fred Caruso *The Pond at Cape May Point*

Basil King *Disparate Beasts: Basil King's Beastiary, Part Two; 77 Beasts; Disparate Beasts; Mirage; The Spoken Word / The Painted Hand from Learning to Draw / A History*

Martha King *Imperfect Fit*

Phillip Lopate *At the End of the Day: Selected Poems and An Introductory Essay*

Mary Mackey *Breaking the Fever; The Jaguars That Prowl Our Dreams; Sugar Zone; Travelers With No Ticket Home*

Jason McCall *Dear Hero,*

Sandy McIntosh *The After-Death History of My Mother; Between Earth and Sky; Cemetery Chess; Ernesta, in the Style of the Flamenco; Forty-Nine Guaranteed Ways to Escape Death; A Hole In the Ocean; Lesser Lights; Obsessional*

Stephen Paul Miller *Any Lie You Tell Will Be the Truth; The Bee Flies in May; Fort Dad; Skinny Eighth Avenue; There's Only One God and You're Not It*

Daniel Morris *Blue Poles; Bryce Passage; Hit Play; If Not for the Courage*

Gail Newman *Blood Memory*

Geoffrey O'Brien *Where Did Poetry Come From; The Blue Hill*

Sharon Olinka *The Good City*

Christina Olivares *No Map of the Earth Includes Stars*

Justin Petropoulos *Eminent Domain*

Paul Pines *Charlotte Songs; Divine Madness; Gathering Sparks; Last Call at the Tin Palace*

Jacquelyn Pope *Watermark*

George Quasha *Things Done for Themselves*

Karin Randolph *Either She Was*

Rochelle Ratner *Balancing Acts; Ben Casey Days; House and Home*

Michael Rerick *In Ways Impossible to Fold*

Corrine Robins *Facing It; One Thousand Years; Today's Menu*

Eileen R. Tabios *The Connoisseur of Alleys; I Take Thee, English, for My Beloved; The In(ter)vention of the Hay(na)ku; The Light Sang as It Left Your Eyes; Reproductions of the Empty Flagpole; Sun Stigmata; The Thorn Rosary*

Eileen R. Tabios and j/j hastain *The Relational Elations of Orphaned Algebra*

Susan Terris *Familiar Tense; Ghost of Yesterday; Natural Defenses*

Lynne Thompson *Fretwork*

Madeline Tiger *Birds of Sorrow and Joy*

Tana Jean Welch *Latest Volcano*

Harriet Zinnes: *Drawing on the Wall; Light Light or the Curvature of the Earth; New and Selected Poems; Weather is Whether; Whither Nonstopping*

Tony Trigilio: *Proof Something Happened*

YEAR	AUTHOR	TITLE	JUDGE
2004	Jacquelyn Pope	*Watermark*	Marie Ponsot
2005	Sigman Byrd	*Under the Wanderer's Star*	Gerald Stern
2006	Steve Fellner	*Blind Date with Cavafy*	Denise Duhamel
2007	Karin Randolph	*Either She Was*	David Shapiro
2008	Michael Rerick	*In Ways Impossible to Fold*	Thylias Moss
2009	Neil de la Flor	*Almost Dorothy*	Forrest Gander
2010	Justin Petropoulos	*Eminent Domain*	Anne Waldman
2011	Meredith Cole	*Miniatures*	Alicia Ostriker
2012	Jason McCall	*Dear Hero,*	Cornelius Eady
2013	Tom Beckett	*Dipstick (Diptych)*	Charles Bernstein
2014	Christina Olivares	*No Map of the Earth Includes Stars*	Brenda Hillman
2015	Tana Jean Welch	*Latest Volcano*	Stephanie Strickland
2016	Robert Gibb	*After*	Mark Doty
2017	Geoffrey O'Brien	*The Blue Hill*	Meena Alexander
2018	Lynne Thompson	*Fretwork*	Jane Hirshfield
2019	Gail Newman	*Blood Memory*	Marge Piercy
2020	Tony Trigilio	*Proof Something Happened*	Susan Howe

ARTISTIC ADVISORY BOARD

Toi Derricotte, Denise Duhamel, Marilyn Hacker, Allan Kornblum (in memorium), Maria Mazzioti Gillan, Alicia Ostriker, Marie Ponsot (in memorium), David Shapiro, Nathaniel Tarn, Anne Waldman, and John Yau.
For more information, please go to: www.marshhawkpress.org